I0490887

Digital Marketing Success:
Expert Strategies and Case Studies for Online Entrepreneurs

Dan M. Savage

Table of contents

Chapter 1

Understanding the Basics of Digital Marketing

In today's digital age, businesses must have an online presence to succeed. Digital marketing has become an essential tool for businesses of all sizes and types to reach their target audience, increase brand awareness, and drive sales. In this chapter, we will explore the basics of digital marketing, including what it is, its benefits, and different types of digital marketing.

What is Digital Marketing?

Digital marketing is the use of digital channels, such as search engines, social media, email, mobile apps, and websites, to promote products, services, or brands. It involves a range of tactics and strategies that aim to create and maintain a connection with potential and existing customers in the online space.

The Benefits of Digital Marketing

Increased Reach: Digital marketing allows businesses to reach a wider audience than traditional marketing methods. With billions of people using the internet every day, businesses can use digital marketing to target and engage with potential customers from all over the world.

Cost-effective: Compared to traditional marketing methods, digital marketing is often more cost-effective. It allows businesses to reach a larger audience without spending a lot of money on print, radio, or television advertisements.

Measurable Results: Digital marketing provides measurable results, which allows businesses to track their progress and adjust their strategies accordingly. Metrics such as website traffic, engagement rates, and conversion rates can be easily tracked and analyzed to determine the effectiveness of marketing campaigns.

Targeted Advertising: Digital marketing allows businesses to target specific audiences based on demographics, interests, behaviors, and location. This targeting ensures that marketing efforts are focused on those who are most likely to convert into customers.

Increased Brand Awareness: Digital marketing allows businesses to increase their brand awareness by creating and sharing content across various digital channels. This content can include blog posts, social media updates, infographics, videos, and more.

Different Types of Digital Marketing

Search Engine Optimization (SEO): SEO is the practice of optimizing a website's content to improve its visibility and ranking on search engines such as Google, Bing, and Yahoo. It involves keyword research, content creation, link building, and website optimization.

Pay-per-click Advertising (PPC): PPC is a type of advertising where businesses pay each time a user clicks on one of their ads. Ads are typically displayed on search engines, social media platforms, or websites, and businesses bid on keywords to ensure their ads appear in front of the right audience.

Social Media Marketing: Social media marketing involves creating and sharing content on social media platforms such as Facebook, Twitter, Instagram, and LinkedIn. The goal is to engage with the target audience and drive traffic to a website or landing page.

Content Marketing: Content marketing involves creating and sharing valuable content, such as blog posts, videos, and infographics, to attract and engage with the target audience. The goal is to build trust, authority, and credibility with potential customers.

Email Marketing: Email marketing involves sending emails to a list of subscribers to promote products, services, or events. The goal is to nurture leads and build a relationship with potential customers.

Conclusion

Digital marketing is a powerful tool for businesses of all sizes and types to reach their target audience, increase brand awareness, and drive sales. By understanding the basics of digital marketing, businesses can create effective marketing strategies that leverage the power of digital channels to connect with potential customers and grow their business.

Chapter Summary

- Digital marketing uses digital channels to promote products, services, or brands to potential and existing customers in the online space

- It provides benefits such as increased reach, cost-effectiveness, measurable results, targeted advertising, and increased brand awareness

- Different types of digital marketing include search engine optimization (SEO), pay-per-click advertising (PPC), social media marketing, content marketing, and email marketing

- Businesses can create effective digital marketing strategies by understanding these basics and leveraging the power of digital channels to connect with potential customers and grow their business.

Chapter 2

Developing an Effective Digital Marketing Strategy

Developing an effective digital marketing strategy is essential for any business that wants to succeed in the digital world. This chapter will explore the key components of an effective digital marketing strategy, including conducting a SWOT analysis, identifying the target audience, setting SMART goals, and defining Key Performance Indicators (KPIs).

Conducting a SWOT Analysis

Before developing a digital marketing strategy, it's crucial to conduct a SWOT analysis. SWOT stands for Strengths, Weaknesses, Opportunities, and Threats. A SWOT analysis helps businesses identify their internal strengths and weaknesses and external opportunities and threats.

Strengths: What does your business do well? What sets you apart from your competitors?

Weaknesses: What areas does your business need to improve? What are your competitors doing better than you?

Opportunities: What trends or changes in the market could benefit your business? Are there any untapped markets that you could target?

Threats: What challenges or obstacles could prevent your business from succeeding? What are your competitors doing that could harm your business?

Identifying the Target Audience

Once you've completed your SWOT analysis, the next step is to identify your target audience. Who are you trying to reach with your digital marketing efforts? What are their needs, wants, and pain points? By understanding your target audience, you can tailor your digital marketing strategy to meet their needs and effectively reach them.

Setting SMART Goals

To create an effective digital marketing strategy, you need to set SMART goals. SMART stands for Specific, Measurable, Attainable, Relevant, and Time-bound. Here's how to set SMART goals:

Specific: Define what you want to achieve with your digital marketing efforts. For example, you might want to increase website traffic or generate more leads.

Measurable: Define how you will measure the success of your digital marketing efforts. For example, you might track website traffic, conversion rates, or social media engagement.

Attainable: Make sure your goals are realistic and achievable within your budget and resources.

Relevant: Ensure that your goals align with your business objectives and overall marketing strategy.

Time-bound: Define a specific timeframe for achieving your goals, such as six months or one year.

Defining Key Performance Indicators (KPIs)

Once you've set your SMART goals, you need to define Key Performance Indicators (KPIs) to track your progress. KPIs are specific metrics that you can use to measure the success of your digital marketing efforts. Examples of KPIs include website traffic, conversion rates, social media engagement, and email open rates. By tracking your KPIs, you can determine what's working and what's not and make data-driven decisions to optimize your digital marketing strategy.

Conclusion

Developing an effective digital marketing strategy requires conducting a SWOT analysis, identifying your target audience, setting SMART goals, and defining Key Performance Indicators (KPIs). By following these key components, you can create a digital marketing strategy that aligns with your business objectives, targets the right audience, and drives measurable results.

Chapter Summary

- Developing an effective digital marketing strategy is crucial for business success in the digital world.

- Conducting a SWOT analysis is important to identify internal strengths and weaknesses and external opportunities and threats.

- Identifying the target audience helps tailor digital marketing strategies to meet their needs.

- Setting SMART goals - specific, measurable, attainable, relevant, and time-bound - is necessary to create an effective digital marketing strategy.

- Defining Key Performance Indicators (KPIs) allows businesses to track progress and make data-driven decisions to optimize their digital marketing strategy.

Chapter 3

Search Engine Optimization (SEO)

Search engine optimization (SEO) is the practice of optimizing a website to improve its visibility and ranking in search engine results pages (SERPs). This chapter will explore the key concepts of SEO, including how search engines work, on-page and off-page optimization, keyword research and optimization, and link building strategies.

Understanding How Search Engines Work

Search engines use complex algorithms to determine the relevance and authority of a website to specific search queries. The process involves crawling and indexing web pages, analyzing content, and ranking results based on factors such as relevance, authority, and user experience. SEO aims to optimize websites for these factors, improving their visibility and ranking in SERPs.

On-Page and Off-Page Optimization

On-page optimization involves optimizing a website's content and structure to improve its relevance and authority for specific keywords. This includes optimizing meta tags, headlines, images, and content for target keywords, as well as improving the website's user experience, loading speed, and mobile-friendliness.

Off-page optimization involves optimizing external factors that influence a website's ranking, such as backlinks and social media signals. This includes building high-quality backlinks from authoritative websites and social media platforms, as well as engaging with users on social media to build brand awareness and authority.

Keyword Research and Optimization

Keyword research is the process of identifying the most relevant and profitable keywords for a business's target audience. This includes researching the search volume, competition, and intent behind specific keywords, as well as identifying long-tail keywords that are more specific and less competitive.

Keyword optimization involves using these keywords strategically throughout a website's content and structure, including in meta tags, headlines, content, and image alt tags. However, it is important to use keywords naturally and not overuse them, as this can result in a penalty from search engines.

Link Building Strategies

Link building is the process of acquiring high-quality backlinks from other websites to improve a website's authority and relevance for specific keywords. There are several link building strategies, including guest blogging, broken link building, and social media outreach.

Guest blogging involves writing high-quality content for other websites in exchange for a backlink to your website. Broken link building involves finding broken links on other websites and offering a replacement link to your website. Social media outreach involves engaging with users on social media platforms and building relationships that can lead to backlinks and social media shares.

Conclusion

In conclusion, SEO is a complex and ever-evolving practice that involves optimizing a website for search engines and user experience. By understanding how search engines work, implementing on-page and off-page optimization strategies, conducting keyword research and optimization, and using effective link building strategies, businesses can improve their website's visibility and ranking in SERPs, driving organic traffic and ultimately achieving their digital marketing goals.

Chapter Summary

- SEO is the practice of optimizing a website to improve its visibility and ranking in search engine results pages (SERPs).

- Search engines use complex algorithms to determine the relevance and authority of a website to specific search queries.

- On-page optimization involves optimizing a website's content and structure, while off-page optimization involves optimizing external factors that influence a website's ranking, such as backlinks and social media signals.

- Keyword research and optimization involve identifying the most relevant and profitable keywords for a business's target audience and using them strategically throughout a website's content and structure.

- Link building is the process of acquiring high-quality backlinks from other websites to improve a website's authority and relevance for specific keywords.

- Effective link building strategies include guest blogging, broken link building, and social media outreach.

- By implementing these SEO strategies, businesses can improve their website's visibility and ranking in SERPs, driving organic traffic and achieving their digital marketing goals.

Chapter 4

Pay-Per-Click (PPC) Advertising

Pay-per-click (PPC) advertising is a popular digital marketing strategy that involves placing ads on search engine results pages (SERPs) and paying each time a user clicks on the ad. This chapter will explore the key elements of PPC advertising, including understanding the basics, developing effective ad campaigns, identifying the right keywords, and optimizing landing pages.

Understanding the Basics of PPC Advertising

PPC advertising is a form of online advertising that allows businesses to reach their target audience by placing ads on search engines like Google and Bing. Advertisers bid on keywords that users search for, and their ads are displayed on the search engine results page when the user enters the relevant search terms. The advertiser only pays when a user clicks on the ad, hence the term "pay-per-click."

Developing Effective Ad Campaigns

Developing an effective PPC ad campaign involves several key steps. This includes setting campaign goals, creating compelling ad copy, selecting the right keywords, targeting the right audience, and optimizing ad campaigns over time. Advertisers must continually monitor and adjust their ad campaigns to ensure they are achieving their desired results.

Identifying the Right Keywords

Identifying the right keywords is critical to the success of a PPC ad campaign. This involves researching and selecting keywords that are relevant to the business and its target audience. Advertisers must also consider the competition for each keyword and adjust their bids accordingly to ensure their ads appear in the top search results.

Optimizing Landing Pages

Optimizing landing pages is another critical element of PPC advertising. A landing page is the page on a website that a user is directed to after clicking on an ad. Landing pages must be optimized to ensure they align with the ad copy and provide users with relevant information. The landing page should also include a clear call-to-action to encourage users to take the desired action, such as filling out a form or making a purchase.

Conclusion

PPC advertising is an effective way for businesses to reach their target audience and drive conversions. By understanding the basics of PPC advertising, developing effective ad campaigns, identifying the right keywords, and optimizing landing pages, businesses can achieve success in their digital marketing efforts. It is essential to continually monitor and adjust ad campaigns over time to ensure they are achieving their desired results. With a solid PPC advertising strategy in place, businesses can attract more qualified leads and ultimately achieve their business goals.

Chapter Summary

- PPC advertising involves placing ads on search engines and paying each time a user clicks on the ad.

- Effective ad campaigns involve setting goals, creating compelling ad copy, selecting the right keywords, targeting the right audience, and optimizing campaigns over time.

- Identifying the right keywords is critical to the success of a PPC ad campaign, and advertisers must adjust their bids based on competition.

- Landing pages must be optimized to align with ad copy, provide relevant information, and include a clear call-to-action.

- Continual monitoring and adjustment of PPC ad campaigns is essential for success

- PPC advertising can help businesses reach their target audience and achieve their business goals.

Chapter 5

Social Media Marketing

Social media marketing is the use of social media platforms to promote a business and its products or services. This chapter will explore the key elements of social media marketing, including understanding social media platforms, creating effective social media strategies, developing engaging content, and measuring social media ROI.

Understanding Social Media Platforms

Social media platforms are websites and applications that enable users to create and share content or participate in social networking. Some popular social media platforms include Facebook, Instagram, Twitter, LinkedIn, and TikTok. Each platform has its unique features and audience, making it essential for businesses to understand each platform's strengths and limitations to create an effective social media marketing strategy.

Creating Effective Social Media Strategies

Creating an effective social media marketing strategy involves setting clear goals, identifying the target audience, creating a content calendar, and selecting appropriate platforms. The strategy should be focused on building brand awareness, engaging with customers, and driving traffic to the website. It should also be flexible enough to adapt to changing trends and audience needs.

Developing Engaging Content

Developing engaging content is essential to the success of social media marketing. The content should be tailored to each platform, resonate with the target audience, and be visually appealing. Types of content can include images, videos, infographics, blog posts, and user-generated content. It is also essential to engage with the audience by responding to comments and messages promptly.

Measuring Social Media ROI

Measuring social media ROI is essential to understand the effectiveness of the social media marketing strategy. Metrics to track can include reach, engagement, website traffic, and conversions. It is also essential to monitor the competition and adjust the strategy accordingly.

Conclusion

Social media marketing is a powerful tool for businesses to connect with their audience, build brand awareness, and drive traffic to the website. By understanding social media platforms, creating effective social media strategies, developing engaging content, and measuring social media ROI, businesses can create a successful social media marketing strategy. With a solid social media marketing strategy in place, businesses can achieve their marketing goals, increase brand loyalty, and drive conversions.

Chapter Summary

- Social media marketing uses social media platforms to promote a business and its products or services.

- Understanding social media platforms is crucial to creating an effective social media marketing strategy.

- Effective social media strategies involve clear goals, identifying target audiences, creating content calendars, and selecting appropriate platforms.

- Developing engaging content tailored to each platform is essential for success.

- Measuring social media ROI is essential to understand the effectiveness of the strategy.

- Metrics to track can include reach, engagement, website traffic, and conversions.

- With a solid social media marketing strategy in place, businesses can achieve their marketing goals, increase brand loyalty, and drive conversions.

Chapter 6

Email Marketing

Email marketing is the practice of sending targeted, personalized messages to a list of subscribers to promote a business, its products or services. This chapter will explore the key elements of email marketing, including understanding the benefits of email marketing, creating effective email campaigns, segmenting email lists, and measuring email marketing ROI.

Understanding the Benefits of Email Marketing

Email marketing has several benefits for businesses, including increased customer engagement, building brand loyalty, and generating leads. It is also a cost-effective marketing strategy that can reach a large audience with minimal effort. Email marketing is a valuable tool for businesses to stay connected with their customers, drive conversions, and increase revenue.

Creating Effective Email Campaigns

Creating effective email campaigns involves developing a clear message, selecting appropriate visuals, and using personalization to engage with the audience. The content should be tailored to the recipient's interests, and the subject line should be attention-grabbing. It is also essential to include a clear call to action that directs the recipient to take the desired action.

Segmenting Email Lists

Segmenting email lists involves dividing the subscriber list into smaller groups based on demographics, interests, or behavior. This allows businesses to tailor their message to specific segments of the audience, resulting in higher open rates and conversions. Segmentation can be based on factors such as age, location, purchase history, and engagement level.

Measuring Email Marketing ROI

Measuring email marketing ROI involves tracking metrics such as open rates, click-through rates, conversion rates, and revenue generated. This allows businesses to determine the effectiveness of their email marketing campaigns and make data-driven decisions to improve future campaigns. It is also essential to monitor the competition and adjust the strategy accordingly.

Conclusion

Email marketing is a powerful tool for businesses to engage with their audience, promote their products or services, and drive conversions. By understanding the benefits of email marketing, creating effective email campaigns, segmenting email lists, and measuring email marketing ROI, businesses can create a successful email marketing strategy. With a solid email marketing strategy in place, businesses can increase customer engagement, build brand loyalty, and drive revenue.

Chapter Summary

- Email marketing involves sending targeted, personalized messages to subscribers to promote a business and its products or services.

- Benefits of email marketing include increased customer engagement, building brand loyalty, and generating leads.

- Effective email campaigns involve developing a clear message, selecting appropriate visuals, and using personalization to engage with the audience.

- Segmentation of email lists allows businesses to tailor messages to specific segments of the audience, resulting in higher open rates and conversions.

- Measuring email marketing ROI involves tracking metrics such as open rates, click-through rates, conversion rates, and revenue generated.

- Email marketing is a cost-effective strategy that can reach a large audience with minimal effort.

- With a solid email marketing strategy in place, businesses can increase customer engagement, build brand loyalty, and drive revenue.

Chapter 7

Content Marketing

Content marketing is a digital marketing strategy that involves creating and sharing valuable, relevant, and consistent content to attract and retain a clearly defined audience. This chapter will explore the key elements of content marketing, including understanding the importance of content marketing, creating a content marketing plan, developing high-quality content, and measuring content marketing ROI.

Understanding the Importance of Content Marketing

Content marketing is essential to building brand awareness, driving traffic to the website, and establishing a relationship with the audience. By providing valuable content, businesses can establish themselves as thought leaders in their industry and increase their credibility. Content marketing also helps businesses connect with their audience on a personal level, building trust and loyalty.

Creating a Content Marketing Plan

Creating a content marketing plan involves defining goals, identifying the target audience, creating a content calendar, and selecting appropriate channels to promote the content. The plan should be flexible enough to adapt to changing trends and audience needs. It should also be focused on creating content that is valuable, informative, and relevant to the audience.

Developing High-Quality Content

Developing high-quality content is essential to the success of content marketing. The content should be visually appealing, well-written, and easy to understand. Types of content can include blog posts, videos, infographics, whitepapers, and e-books. It is also essential to promote the content on social media, email, and other channels to increase its reach.

Measuring Content Marketing ROI

Measuring content marketing ROI is essential to understand the effectiveness of the content marketing strategy. Metrics to track can include website traffic, engagement, lead generation, and revenue generated. It is also important to track the performance of individual pieces of content to understand what types of content are resonating with the audience.

Conclusion

Content marketing is a powerful tool for businesses to connect with their audience, build brand awareness, and drive traffic to the website. By understanding the importance of content marketing, creating a content marketing plan, developing high-quality content, and measuring content marketing ROI, businesses can create a successful content marketing strategy. With a solid content marketing strategy in place, businesses can increase their ROI, establish themselves as thought leaders, and achieve their marketing goals.

Chapter Summary

- Content marketing involves creating and sharing valuable and relevant content to attract and retain a defined audience.

- The importance of content marketing includes building brand awareness, driving website traffic, and establishing relationships with the audience.

- A content marketing plan involves defining goals, identifying the target audience, creating a content calendar, and selecting appropriate channels to promote the content.

- Developing high-quality content is crucial for success, and it should be visually appealing, well-written, and easy to understand.

- Measuring content marketing ROI involves tracking metrics such as website traffic, engagement, lead generation, and revenue generated.

- A successful content marketing strategy can help businesses connect with their audience, build brand awareness, and achieve their marketing goals.

Chapter 8

Analytics and Metrics

Analytics and metrics are essential to understanding the effectiveness of digital marketing campaigns. This chapter will explore the key elements of analytics and metrics, including understanding the importance of analytics, measuring the effectiveness of digital marketing campaigns, identifying key performance indicators (KPIs), and using analytics to optimize campaigns.

Understanding the Importance of Analytics

Analytics is the process of collecting, measuring, and analyzing data to understand user behavior, website performance, and digital marketing campaign effectiveness. Analytics is essential to understanding what is working and what is not, and identifying opportunities for improvement. Without analytics, businesses are operating blindly and missing opportunities for growth and optimization.

Measuring the Effectiveness of Digital Marketing Campaigns

Measuring the effectiveness of digital marketing campaigns involves tracking a variety of metrics, including website traffic, conversion rates, engagement, and revenue generated. These metrics can help businesses understand which campaigns are driving the most traffic, generating the most leads, and converting the most customers. It is important to track these metrics over time to identify trends and patterns.

Identifying Key Performance Indicators (KPIs)

Identifying key performance indicators (KPIs) is essential to understanding the success of digital marketing campaigns. KPIs are specific, measurable, and time-bound goals that businesses set to evaluate the success of their marketing efforts. Examples of KPIs include website traffic, conversion rates, click-through rates, and revenue generated. Identifying KPIs helps businesses stay focused on what is important and prioritize their marketing efforts accordingly.

Using Analytics to Optimize Campaigns

Using analytics to optimize campaigns involves analyzing data to identify opportunities for improvement and testing new strategies to improve performance. For example, businesses can use A/B testing to test different ad copy or landing pages to see which version performs better. By continuously testing and analyzing data, businesses can improve their marketing performance and achieve their goals more efficiently.

Conclusion

Analytics and metrics are essential to understanding the effectiveness of digital marketing campaigns. By understanding the importance of analytics, measuring the effectiveness of digital marketing campaigns, identifying key performance indicators (KPIs), and using analytics to optimize campaigns, businesses can improve their marketing performance and achieve their goals more efficiently. With a data-driven approach to marketing, businesses can stay ahead of the competition and drive growth and success.

Chapter Summary

- Analytics and metrics are essential to understand the effectiveness of digital marketing campaigns.

- Analytics helps to understand user behavior, website performance, and campaign effectiveness.

- Measuring campaign effectiveness involves tracking metrics such as website traffic, conversion rates, and revenue generated.

- Identifying key performance indicators (KPIs) is essential to understanding the success of campaigns.

- KPIs are specific, measurable, and time-bound goals that help businesses evaluate the success of their marketing efforts.

- Using analytics to optimize campaigns involves analyzing data to identify opportunities for improvement and testing new strategies to improve performance.

- A data-driven approach to marketing can help businesses stay ahead of the competition and drive growth and success.

Chapter 9

Case Studies and Success Stories

Case studies and success stories provide valuable insights into what works and what doesn't in digital marketing. This chapter will explore the key elements of case studies and success stories, including examining successful digital marketing campaigns, analyzing the strategies behind successful campaigns, and learning from other businesses' successes and failures.

Examining Successful Digital Marketing Campaigns

Examining successful digital marketing campaigns involves looking at campaigns that have achieved significant success in terms of website traffic, conversion rates, and revenue generated. Case studies and success stories can provide valuable insights into the strategies and tactics that were used to achieve this success. Examples of successful digital marketing campaigns include the Old Spice "Smell Like a Man, Man" campaign, the Dollar Shave Club viral video, and the Airbnb "Live There" campaign.

Analyzing the Strategies Behind Successful Campaigns

Analyzing the strategies behind successful campaigns involves looking at the tactics that were used to achieve the campaign's objectives. This can include analyzing the targeting, messaging, creative, and distribution channels used. It is important to identify what worked well and what didn't, and to understand how these tactics contributed to the campaign's success. For example, the Old Spice campaign's use of humor, celebrity endorsements, and social media engagement contributed to its success.

Learning from Other Businesses' Successes and Failures

Learning from other businesses' successes and failures involves understanding what strategies and tactics have worked well for other businesses in your industry, as well as what mistakes they have made. This can provide valuable insights into what you can do to achieve success, as well as what pitfalls to avoid. It is important to keep an open mind and be willing to try new things, while also learning from the experiences of others.

Conclusion

Case studies and success stories provide valuable insights into what works and what doesn't in digital marketing. By examining successful digital marketing campaigns, analyzing the strategies behind successful campaigns, and learning from other businesses' successes and failures, businesses can gain a deeper understanding of how to achieve their marketing goals. With a willingness to learn from others and a commitment to continuous improvement, businesses can achieve success in the ever-evolving world of digital marketing.

Chapter Summary

- Case studies and success stories provide valuable insights into what works and what doesn't in digital marketing.

- Examining successful digital marketing campaigns involves looking at campaigns that have achieved significant success in terms of website traffic, conversion rates, and revenue generated.

- Analyzing the strategies behind successful campaigns involves looking at the tactics that were used to achieve the campaign's objectives, including analyzing the targeting, messaging, creative, and distribution channels used.

- Learning from other businesses' successes and failures involves understanding what strategies and tactics have worked well for other businesses in your industry, as well as what mistakes they have made.

- Businesses can gain a deeper understanding of how to achieve their marketing goals by examining successful digital marketing campaigns, analyzing the strategies behind successful campaigns, and learning from other businesses' successes and failures.

Chapter 10

Tools and Resources

Digital marketing requires a variety of tools and resources to be successful. This chapter will explore the key tools and resources that businesses can use to optimize their digital marketing efforts, including identifying useful tools and resources, understanding the role of marketing automation tools, exploring industry blogs and publications, and participating in industry events and webinars.

Identifying Useful Tools and Resources for Digital Marketing

There are a variety of tools and resources that businesses can use to optimize their digital marketing efforts. These include SEO tools like Google Analytics and SEMrush, social media management tools like Hootsuite and Sprout Social, email marketing tools like Mailchimp and Constant Contact, and content marketing tools like BuzzSumo and CoSchedule. By using these tools, businesses can track their progress, identify opportunities for improvement, and optimize their marketing efforts for success.

Understanding the Role of Marketing Automation Tools

Marketing automation tools are software platforms that help businesses automate their marketing tasks and workflows. These tools can help businesses streamline their processes, save time and resources, and improve their ROI. Examples of marketing automation tools include Hubspot, Marketo, and Pardot. By using these tools, businesses can create targeted campaigns, nurture leads, and track their progress over time.

Exploring Industry Blogs and Publications

Industry blogs and publications are a great resource for staying up-to-date on the latest trends and best practices in digital marketing. Some popular blogs and publications include Moz, Search Engine Land, and Social Media Examiner. By regularly reading these publications, businesses can stay informed about the latest developments in digital marketing and apply these insights to their own marketing efforts.

Participating in Industry Events and Webinars

Industry events and webinars are a great way to network with other professionals in the field and learn from experts in digital marketing. Some popular events include the Digital Marketing World Forum, Content Marketing World, and Social Media Week. By attending these events and webinars, businesses can stay up-to-date on the latest trends and best practices in digital marketing and gain valuable insights from industry experts.

Conclusion

Digital marketing requires a variety of tools and resources to be successful. By identifying useful tools and resources, understanding the role of marketing automation tools, exploring industry blogs and publications, and participating in industry events and webinars, businesses can optimize their digital marketing efforts and achieve their goals. With a data-driven approach to marketing and a willingness to learn from others, businesses can drive growth and success in the digital age.

Chapter Summary

- Digital marketing requires a variety of tools and resources to be successful.

- Businesses can use SEO tools, social media management tools, email marketing tools, and content marketing tools to track progress and optimize marketing efforts.

- Marketing automation tools can help automate marketing tasks and workflows, streamline processes, save time and resources, and improve ROI.

- Industry blogs and publications like Moz, Search Engine Land, and Social Media Examiner are great for staying up-to-date on the latest trends and best practices in digital marketing.

- Industry events and webinars like Digital Marketing World Forum, Content Marketing World, and Social Media Week are a great way to network with other professionals and learn from industry experts.

- With a data-driven approach to marketing and a willingness to learn from others, businesses can drive growth and success in the digital age

Chapter 11

Building a Successful Digital Marketing Team

Digital marketing requires a skilled and dedicated team to be successful. This chapter will explore the key components of building a successful digital marketing team, including identifying key roles in a digital marketing team, hiring the right people, developing an effective team culture, and encouraging ongoing learning and development.

Identifying Key Roles in a Digital Marketing Team

A successful digital marketing team requires a variety of roles, each with its own unique set of skills and responsibilities. Some key roles in a digital marketing team include:

Digital Marketing Manager: responsible for overseeing the overall strategy and execution of digital marketing campaigns.

Content Marketing Manager: responsible for developing and executing content marketing strategies, including creating and distributing content across various channels.

SEO Specialist: responsible for optimizing the website and other digital assets for search engines.

Social Media Manager: responsible for managing and executing social media campaigns across various platforms.

Email Marketing Specialist: responsible for developing and executing email marketing campaigns to drive engagement and conversions.

Hiring the Right People

Hiring the right people is crucial for building a successful digital marketing team. This involves identifying the key skills and attributes needed for each role, as well as assessing candidates' experience and qualifications. It's also important to look for individuals who are passionate about digital marketing, are willing to learn and adapt, and can work collaboratively as part of a team.

Developing an Effective Team Culture

An effective team culture is crucial for building a successful digital marketing team. This involves creating a supportive and collaborative environment where team members feel valued and motivated. Some key components of an effective team culture include clear communication, shared goals and values, recognition and rewards, and opportunities for growth and development.

Encouraging Ongoing Learning and Development

Digital marketing is constantly evolving, and it's important for team members to stay up-to-date with the latest trends and best practices. Encouraging ongoing learning and development is crucial for building a successful digital marketing team. This can involve providing training and resources, encouraging attendance at industry events and webinars, and creating opportunities for team members to share their knowledge and insights.

Conclusion

Building a successful digital marketing team requires a clear understanding of key roles, hiring the right people, developing an effective team culture, and encouraging ongoing learning and development. By investing in a skilled and dedicated team, businesses can drive growth and success in the digital age. With a focus on collaboration, innovation, and continuous improvement, a successful digital marketing team can help businesses achieve their goals and stay ahead of the competition.

Chapter Summary

- A successful digital marketing team requires various roles such as Digital Marketing Manager, Content Marketing Manager, SEO Specialist, Social Media Manager, and Email Marketing Specialist.

- Hiring the right people involves identifying the necessary skills and assessing their qualifications, experience, passion, and ability to work collaboratively.

- An effective team culture includes clear communication, shared goals and values, recognition and rewards, and opportunities for growth and development.

- Encouraging ongoing learning and development involves providing training and resources, attending industry events and webinars, and creating opportunities for sharing knowledge and insights.

- Building a skilled and dedicated team is crucial for driving growth and success in the digital age.

- A successful digital marketing team focuses on collaboration, innovation, and continuous improvement to achieve business goals and stay ahead of the competition.

Chapter 12

Future Trends and Innovations

Digital marketing is a constantly evolving field, with new technologies and trends emerging all the time. This chapter will explore some of the emerging technologies and trends in digital marketing, predict future trends, identify new opportunities for growth and innovation, and offer advice on preparing for the future of digital marketing.

Exploring Emerging Technologies

Emerging technologies such as artificial intelligence (AI), virtual and augmented reality (VR/AR), and blockchain are already starting to impact the digital marketing landscape. AI is being used to power chatbots and personalized advertising, while VR/AR is being used to create immersive brand experiences. Blockchain is being explored as a way to improve transparency and security in digital advertising. These emerging technologies are likely to become even more widespread in the years to come, so businesses need to stay ahead of the curve to remain competitive.

Predicting Future Trends in Digital Marketing

Predicting future trends in digital marketing is never easy, but there are some emerging trends that are likely to become more prominent in the near future. These include the use of voice search, the rise of visual search, the continued importance of video content, and the growing influence of micro-influencers. Businesses that stay up-to-date with these trends and incorporate them into their marketing strategies are likely to stay ahead of the competition.

Identifying New Opportunities for Growth and Innovation

Digital marketing is a field that is constantly evolving, presenting new opportunities for growth and innovation. Businesses that are willing to experiment with new approaches and technologies are likely to find new ways to connect with customers and drive growth. For example, businesses could explore the use of chatbots to provide personalized customer service, or leverage emerging technologies like VR/AR to create unique brand experiences.

Preparing for the Future of Digital Marketing

Preparing for the future of digital marketing requires a commitment to ongoing learning and experimentation. Businesses need to stay up-to-date with emerging technologies and trends, experiment with new approaches, and be willing to adapt their strategies as the digital marketing landscape evolves. They also need to be willing to invest in new technologies and talent to stay ahead of the curve.

Conclusion

The future of digital marketing is full of exciting possibilities, but it requires businesses to be proactive and forward-thinking. By exploring emerging technologies, predicting future trends, identifying new opportunities for growth and innovation, and preparing for the future, businesses can stay competitive and drive growth in the years to come. With a willingness to experiment and a commitment to ongoing learning and development, businesses can stay ahead of the curve and achieve success in the fast-paced world of digital marketing.

Chapter Summary

- Digital marketing is constantly evolving with new technologies and trends emerging all the time.

- Emerging technologies such as AI, VR/AR, and blockchain are already starting to impact the digital marketing landscape.

- Predicted future trends in digital marketing include the rise of voice and visual search, video content, and the growing influence of micro-influencers.

- Digital marketing presents new opportunities for growth and innovation for businesses that are willing to experiment with new approaches and technologies.

- Preparing for the future of digital marketing requires a commitment to ongoing learning and experimentation, staying up-to-date with emerging technologies and trends, and investing in new technologies and talent to stay ahead of the curve.

www.ingramcontent.com/pod-product-compliance
Lightning Source LLC
Chambersburg PA
CBHW071141220526
45467CB00015B/1674